Drawing Is Fun!

DRAWING
DINOSAURS

W
FRANKLIN WATTS

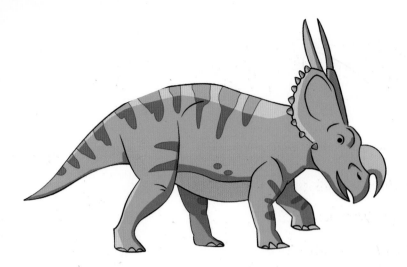

First published in 2012 by Franklin Watts

Copyright © 2012 Arcturus Publishing Limited

Franklin Watts
338 Euston Road
London NW1 3BH

Franklin Watts Australia
Level 17/207 Kent Street, Sydney NSW 2000

Produced by Arcturus Publishing Limited,
26/27 Bickels Yard, 151–153 Bermondsey Street, London SE1 3HA

Cartoon illustrations: Dynamo Limited
Text: Rebecca Clunes and Dynamo Limited
Editors: Anna Brett, Kate Overy and Joe Harris
Design: Tokiko Morishima
Cover design: Tokiko Morishima

Picture credits: All 3D graphics supplied by Shutterstock, except for images on pages 6 and 8,
supplied by iStockphoto.

A CIP catalogue record for this book is available from the British Library.

Dewey Decimal Classification Number 743.8'95679

ISBN 978 1 4451 1021 9

Printed in China

Franklin Watts is a division of Hachette Children's Books, an Hachette UK company.
www.hachette.co.uk

SL001841EN
Supplier 03, Date 0112, Print Run 1430

Contents

Apatosaurus

uh-pah-tuh-SOHR-uhs

This huge dinosaur was about 21 metres (70 feet) long.

Its neck was very long to reach its food.

It ate leaves and bushes growing near the ground.

It used its tail like a whip if a meat-eating dinosaur attacked it.

FUN FACTS ● FUN FACTS ● FUN FACTS ● FUN FACTS ● FUN FACTS

Apatosaurus lived in groups so the adults could keep the babies safe.

1. This shape is the body.

2. Make the neck long and smooth.

3. Put on the head and a long, strong tail.

4. It walks on four strong legs.

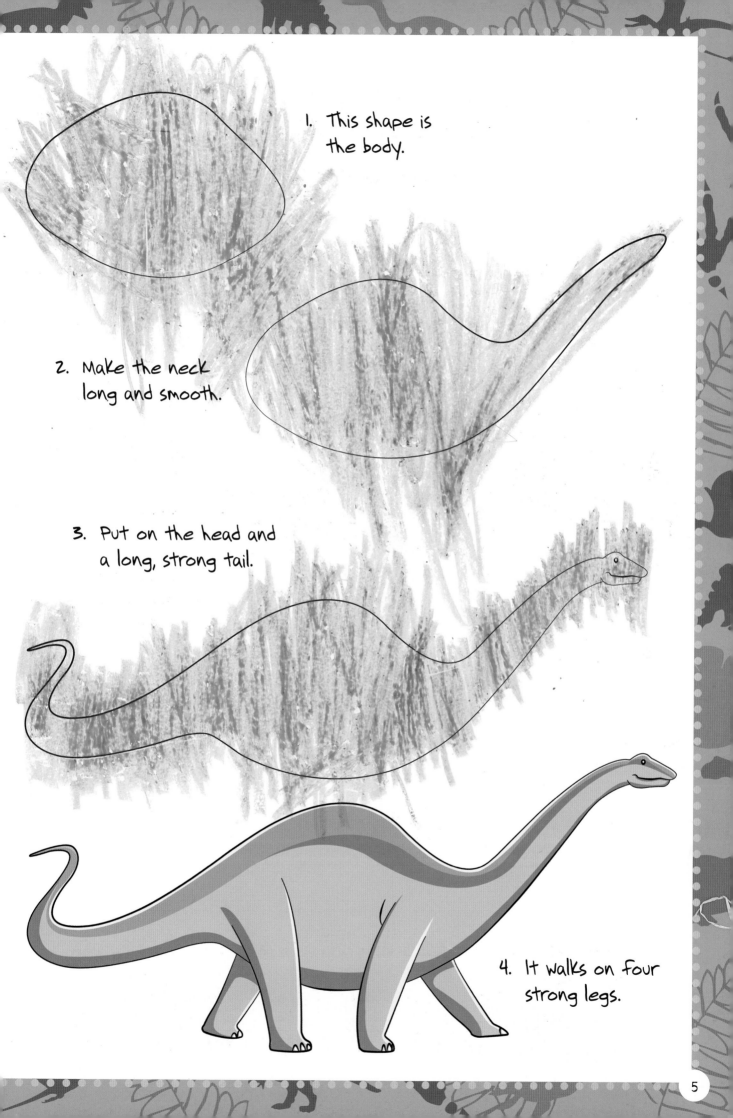

Tyrannosaurus rex

tuh-RA-nuh-SOHR-uhs REHKS

This dinosaur was about 6 metres (20 feet) tall.

Tyrannosaurus rex was one of the biggest meat eaters there has ever been.

It had very sharp teeth.

Its powerful legs helped it to run very fast.

FUN FACTS ● FUN FACTS ● FUN FACTS ● FUN FACTS ● FUN FACTS

Tyrannosaurus rex was so powerful that it could crush bones with its teeth.

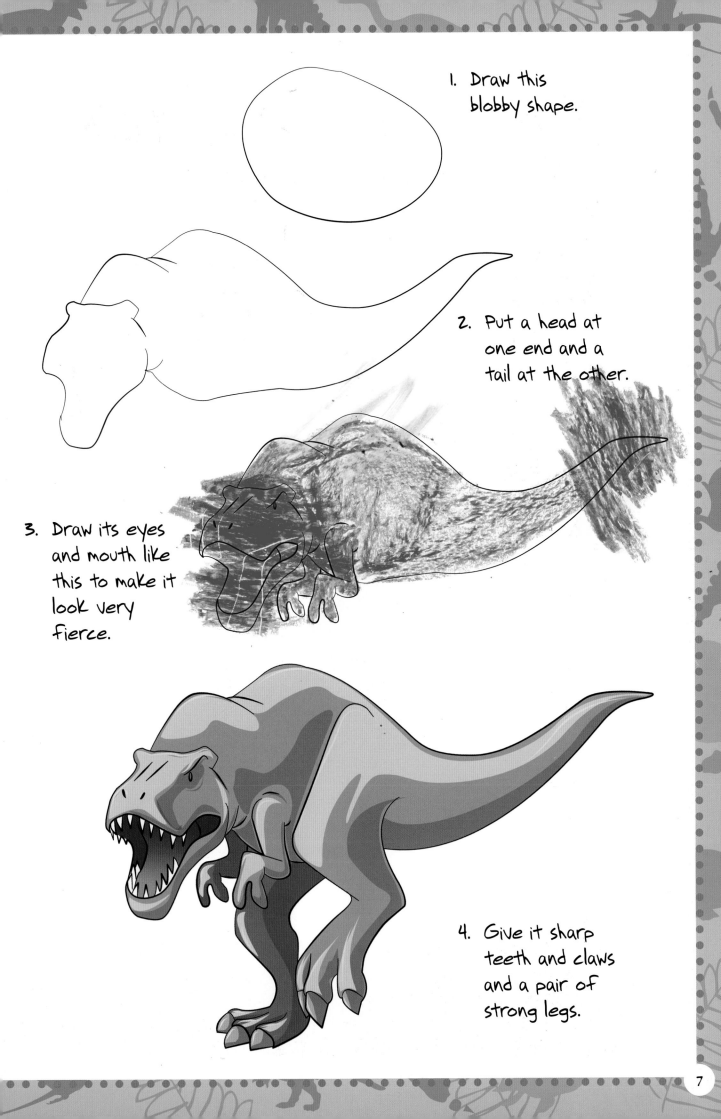

1. Draw this blobby shape.

2. Put a head at one end and a tail at the other.

3. Draw its eyes and mouth like this to make it look very fierce.

4. Give it sharp teeth and claws and a pair of strong legs.

Pteranodon

tuh-RA-nuh-don

Pteranodon lived at the same time as the dinosaurs.

It used its big wings to glide over the sea.

Its wings were tough and leathery.

It scooped up fish in its big mouth.

FUN FACTS ● FUN FACTS ● FUN FACTS ● FUN FACTS ● FUN FACTS

From wing to wing, Pteranodon was nearly 8 metres (25 feet) wide.

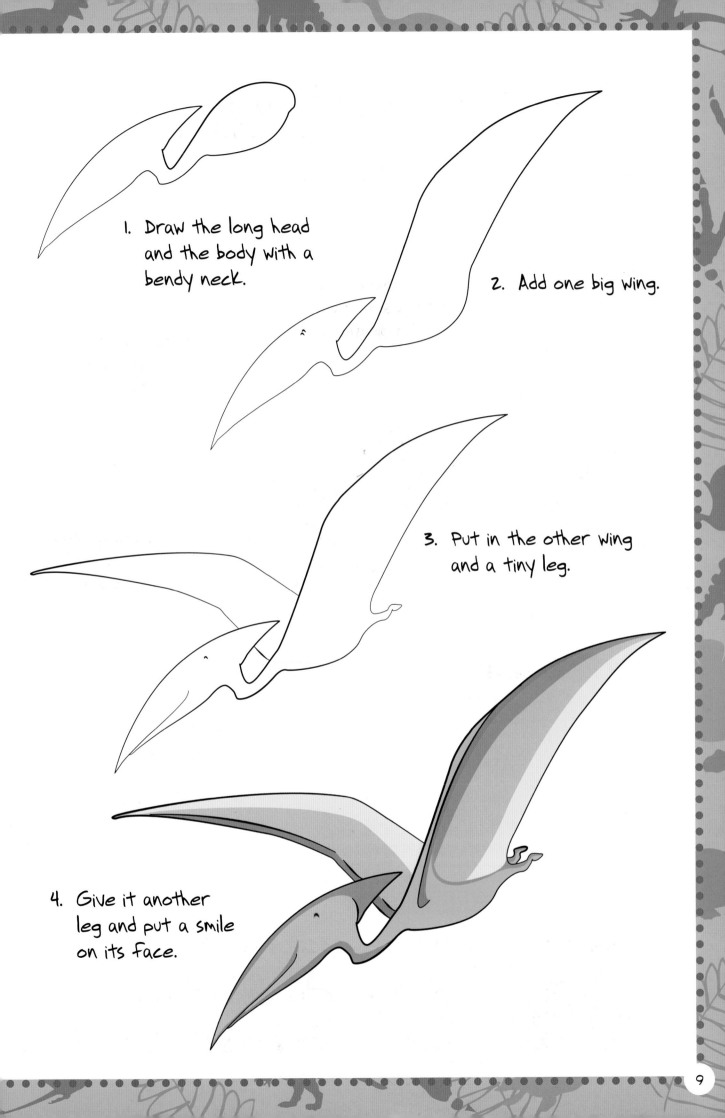

1. Draw the long head and the body with a bendy neck.

2. Add one big wing.

3. Put in the other wing and a tiny leg.

4. Give it another leg and put a smile on its face.

Triceratops

try-SEHR-uh-tops

This dinosaur had two large horns and one smaller horn.

Triceratops was about 9 metres (30 feet) long.

It ate leaves and twigs.

It had strong legs to support its heavy body.

FUN FACTS ● FUN FACTS ● FUN FACTS ● FUN FACTS ● FUN FACTS

Triceratops had a bony plate around its neck to protect it from big meat eaters.

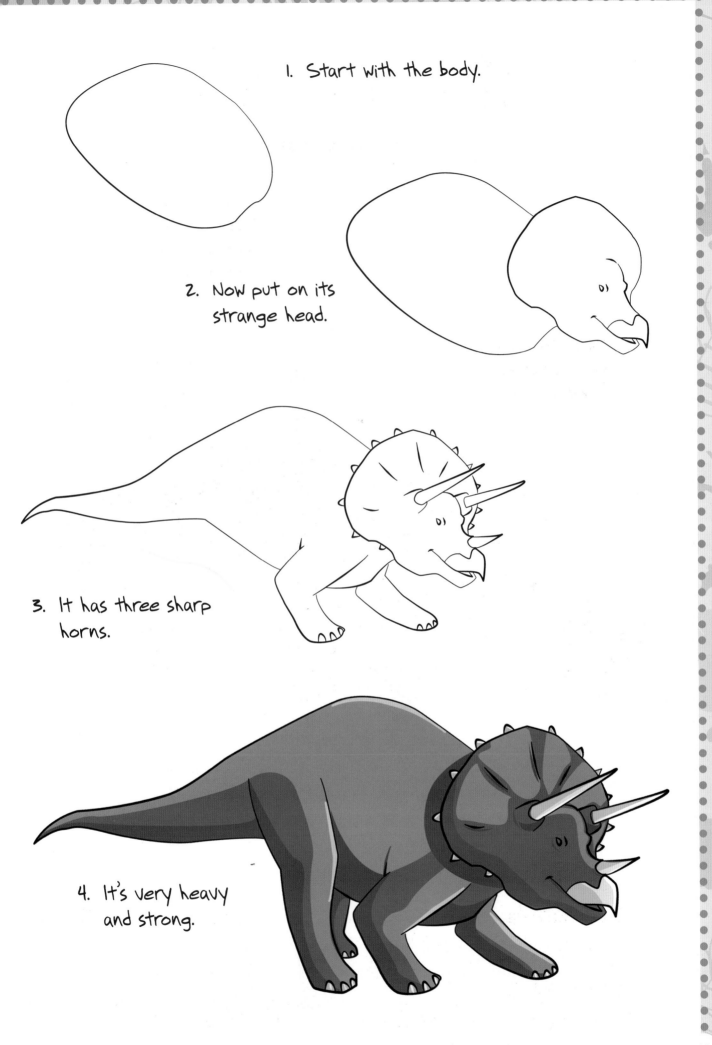

1. Start with the body.

2. Now put on its strange head.

3. It has three sharp horns.

4. It's very heavy and strong.

Archaeopteryx

ahr-kee-OP-tuh-rihks

This was one of the first birds. It lived at the time of the dinosaurs.

It had feathers like a modern bird.

These claws helped it climb around in trees.

It could not fly well, but used its wings to glide.

FUN FACTS ● FUN FACTS ● FUN FACTS ● FUN FACTS ● FUN FACTS

Archaeopteryx was about the size of a pigeon.

1. Draw the body with a feathery tail.

2. Add the head and one large wing.

3. Now add the other wing.

4. Finish it off with legs and clawed feet.

Stegosaurus

steh-guh-SOHR-uhs

This dinosaur ate plants that grew near the ground.

Stegosaurus was about 9 metres (30 feet) long.

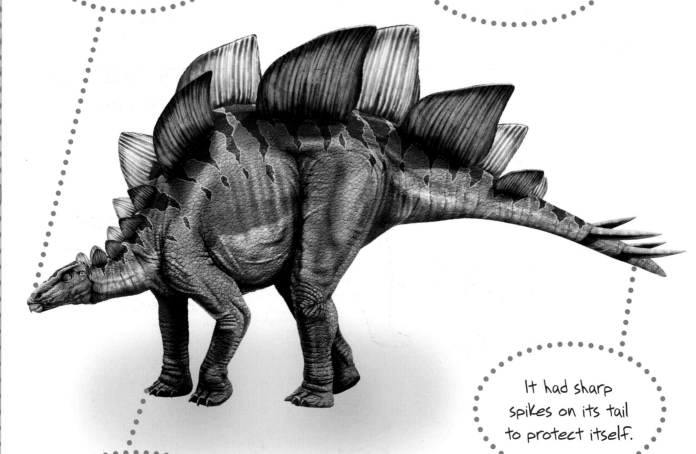

It had sharp spikes on its tail to protect itself.

Its front legs were much shorter than its back legs.

FUN FACTS ● FUN FACTS ● FUN FACTS ● FUN FACTS ● FUN FACTS

Stegosaurus had a very small brain. It was only about the size of a walnut.

1. Draw the body shape.

2. Add the thick neck and tiny head.

3. Now add the four legs.

4. It has big, flat pointed plates on its back.

Deinonychus

dy-NOH-nih-kuhs

This dinosaur had sharp eyes for spotting prey.

Its tail was used for balance as it ran.

Deinonychus was about 3 metres (10 feet) long.

It had large claws on its back feet.

FUN FACTS ● FUN FACTS ● FUN FACTS ● FUN FACTS ● FUN FACTS

Deinonychus hunted in groups. Together they could kill animals much bigger than themselves.

1. Draw a long body to start.

2. Add the head.

3. Give it two small front legs.

4. Add the back legs, then draw its teeth and claws.

Parasaurolophus

pa-ruh-sohr-uh-LOH-fus

This dinosaur had a huge crest on its head.

Parasaurolophus probably lived in groups.

It ate pine needles and other tough leaves.

It could walk on two legs or four legs.

FUN FACTS ● FUN FACTS ● FUN FACTS ● FUN FACTS ● FUN FACTS

Parasaurolophus could blow air through its crest. This made a loud, low noise.

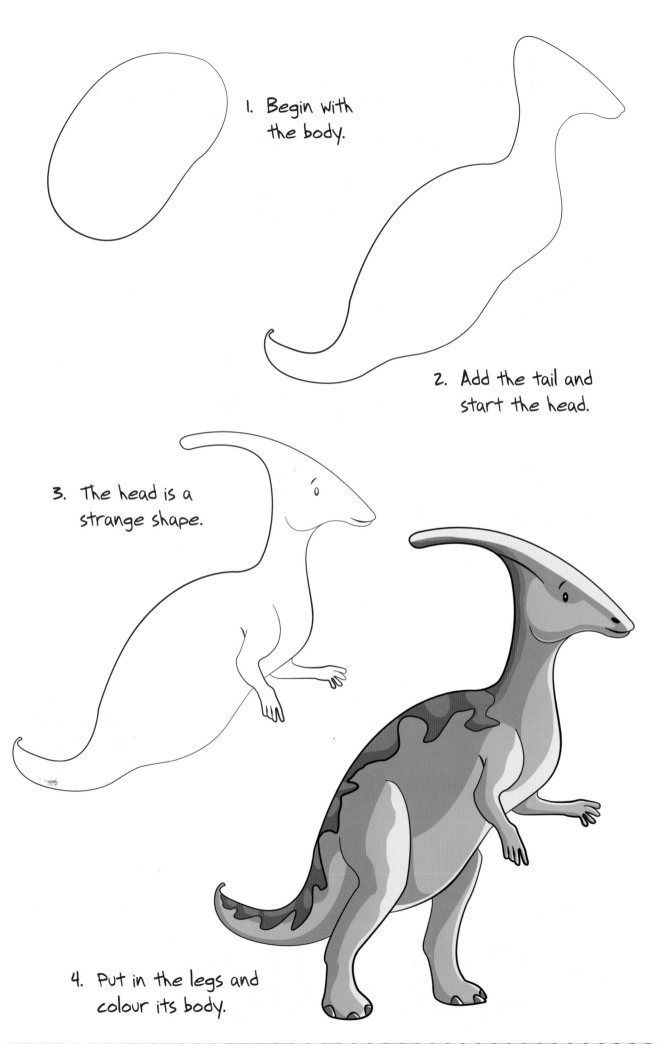

1. Begin with the body.

2. Add the tail and start the head.

3. The head is a strange shape.

4. Put in the legs and colour its body.

Allosaurus

aa-luh-SOHR-uhs

Allosaurus was a meat-eating dinosaur.

Allosaurus was a big dinosaur, almost 12 metres (about 38 feet) long.

It had about 60 very sharp teeth.

It used its front claws to hold onto its prey.

FUN FACTS ● FUN FACTS ● FUN FACTS ● FUN FACTS ● FUN FACTS

Allosaurus ate other dinosaurs. It tried to creep close to them. Then it suddenly attacked.

1. This shape makes the body and the tail.

2. Add the neck and head.

3. Short front arms and eyebrows are next.

4. Powerful back legs finish off this frightening animal.

Brachiosaurus

brah-kee-uh-SOHR-uhs

It used its long neck to reach the leaves at the top of trees.

This huge dinosaur was 23 metres (about 75 feet) long.

It swallowed food without chewing it.

Its front legs were longer than its back legs.

FUN FACTS ● FUN FACTS ● FUN FACTS ● FUN FACTS ● FUN FACTS

A meat-eating dinosaur would not attack an adult Brachiosaurus. It was just too big!

1. A bumpy egg is the starting place for this dinosaur.

2. Give it a long neck and tail.

3. It has thick and powerful front legs.

4. Short back legs help keep this dinosaur on its feet.

Spinosaurus

spy-nuh-SOHR-uhs

Spinosaurus was a meat-eating dinosaur.

The 'sail' on its back was taller than a person.

It snapped up fish with its sharp teeth.

It was more than 11 metres (35 feet) long.

FUN FACTS ● FUN FACTS ● FUN FACTS ● FUN FACTS ● FUN FACTS

Spinosaurus used its sail to keep warm. It stood so the sun shone on its sail. This warmed it up very quickly.

1. Begin with this shape for the body.

2. Add a head with a long mouth, and a powerful tail at the other end.

3. A spiny sail on its back and sharp teeth and claws are next.

4. Now draw the legs. It looks like you may be next for lunch!

Elasmosaurus

ih-laz-muh-SOHR-uhs

Elasmosaurus lived in the seas at the time of the dinosaurs.

Its long neck was used to reach down and snap up fish.

It used its big flippers to swim near the top of the water.

Its neck was as long as its body.

FUN FACTS ● FUN FACTS ● FUN FACTS ● FUN FACTS ● FUN FACTS

Although it spent most of its time in the water, Elasmosaurus breathed air and laid its eggs on land.

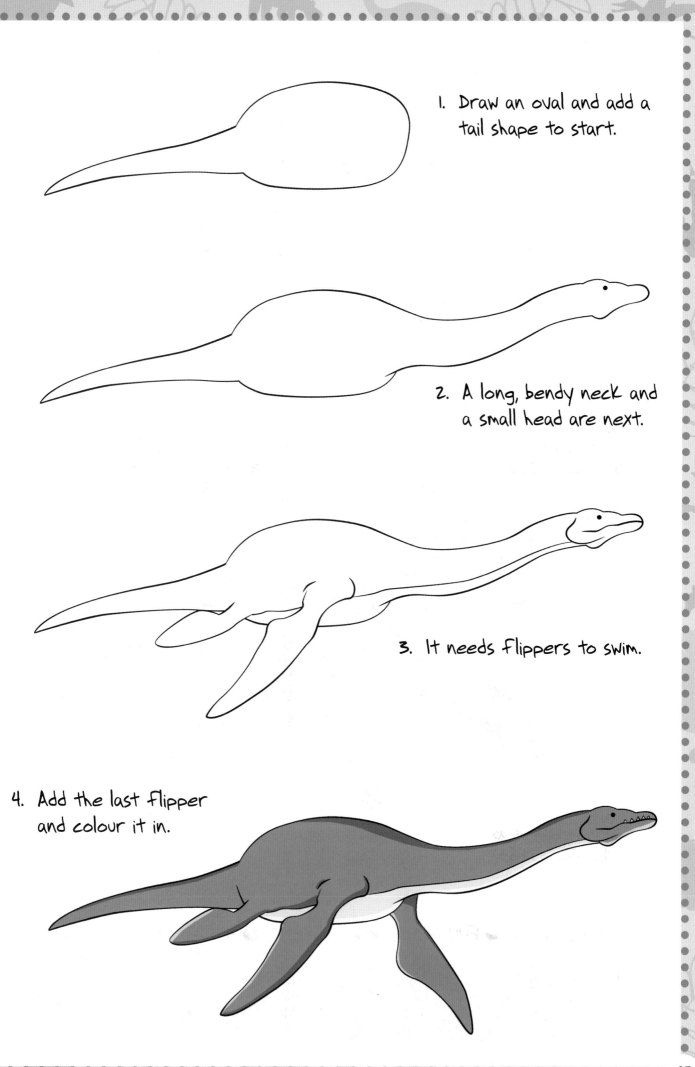

1. Draw an oval and add a tail shape to start.

2. A long, bendy neck and a small head are next.

3. It needs flippers to swim.

4. Add the last flipper and colour it in.

Einiosaurus

eye-nee-uh-SOHR-uhs

This dinosaur ate plants.

It had a huge horn on its nose.

Einiosaurus had two horns to protect its neck.

Einiosaurus fossils have been found in North America.

FUN FACTS ● FUN FACTS ● FUN FACTS ● FUN FACTS ● FUN FACTS

Einiosaurus was about 6 metres (20 feet) long and it probably lived in groups.

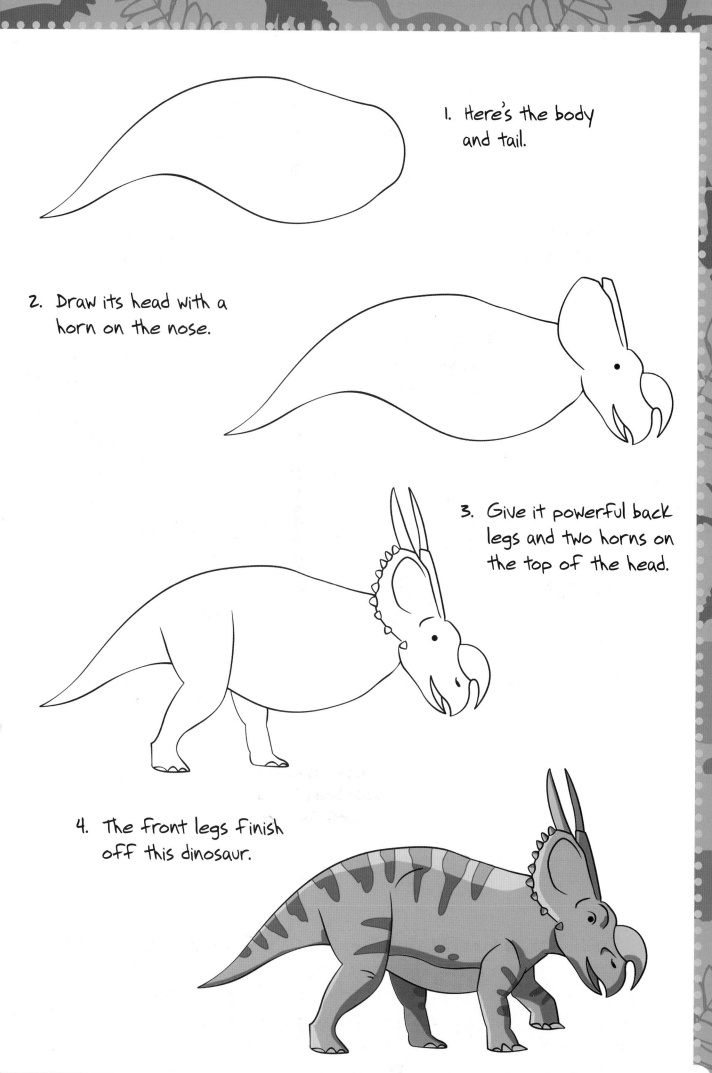

1. Here's the body and tail.

2. Draw its head with a horn on the nose.

3. Give it powerful back legs and two horns on the top of the head.

4. The front legs finish off this dinosaur.

Velociraptor

vuh-LOH-suh-rap-tuhr

This dinosaur was a fierce meat eater.

Its long legs made it a fast runner.

It had long claws on its back feet.

Its front claws were very sharp to grab prey.

FUN FACTS ● FUN FACTS ● FUN FACTS ● FUN FACTS ● FUN FACTS

A fossil has been found of a Velociraptor attacking a plant-eating dinosaur called Protoceratops.

1. Here's the body.

2. Draw the neck and a long, pointy tail.

3. The head and the back legs are next.

4. Put in its front legs and its sharp teeth.

Glossary

balance to stand or move without falling over

bony with skin very near the bone

crest something standing out on top of an animal's head

flipper an animal's leg that is wide and flat, and made for swimming

fossil a rock that shows the shape of an animal or plant from millions of years ago

glide to float through the air for a long time without flapping wings

leathery like tough, thick animal skin

meat eater an animal that eats other animals

plate a hard, wide, flat part of the body

prey the animals that a meat eater kills

scoop to gather up a lot of food at once

spikes sharp points

whip to hit something as if with a long thin rope

Further Reading

Garry Fleming's How to Draw Dinosaurs (The Five Mile Press Pty Ltd, 2010)

How to Draw Dinosaurs by Fiona Watt and Stella Baggott (Usborne Activities, 2005)

How to Draw Dinosaurs and Prehistoric Life by Marit Claridge and Val Biro (Usborne Books, 2006)

It's Fun to Draw Dinosaurs by Mark Bergin (Scribblers, 2011)

Websites

Natural History Museum:
http://www.nhm.ac.uk/kids-only/dinosaurs

BBC Nature Prehistoric Life:
http://www.bbc.co.uk/nature/prehistoric

Dinosaurs for Kids:
http://www.kidsdinos.com

Index

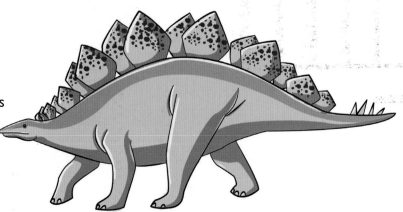